Published in 2022 by Orange Mosquito
An Imprint of Welbeck Children's Limited
part of Welbeck Publishing Group.

Based in London and Sydney.

www.welbeckpublishing.com

In collaboration with Mosquito Books Barcelona S.L.

Design and layout © Mosquito Books Barcelona, SL 2021
Text © Irene Noguer 2021
Illustration © Laura Fernández Arquisola (Laufer) 2021
Translated by Howard Curtis
Publisher: Margaux Durigon
Production: Clare Hennessy

ISBN: 9781914519222
eISBN: 9781914519239

Printed in India

10 9 8 7 6 5 4 3 2 1

Irene Noguer – Laufer

HIDDEN CITIES

Explore Beneath Your Feet and Above your Head

ORANGE

M·O·S·Q·U·I·T·O

RÉSO ⊘

WHERE: Montreal (Canada).

WHY IT WAS BUILT: as protection against extreme winter temperatures, which can reach a freezing -4°F.

INTERESTING FACT: it is the largest underground complex in the world – with more than 18.5 miles of walkway. Here, you can find and do practically everything you do above ground. There are hotels, banks, restaurants, offices, galleries, shops, railway and metro stations, cinemas, discos, and even a library. 12% of the businesses in the center of the city are found here. It used to be known as the Underground City. In 2004 it was renamed RÉSO which is from the French word *réseau* (meaning "network").

ART SOUTERRAIN

Once a year, RÉSO is transformed into a huge art gallery. As part of the "Art Souterrain" ("Underground Art") festival, it is covered in works of art. Going underground, we come across exhibitions on every floor, in a gallery open to all.

ACCESS POINTS

It's easy to descend into RÉSO through one of the 120 external access points found in residential and commercial buildings and through public transport hubs. Once inside, you could spend a whole day here, or even several days, without coming up to the surface!

Although the inhabitants of Montreal use RÉSO to escape extreme cold, this fascinating city is a tourist attraction for visitors from around the world.

SIGNAGE

More than 500,000 pedestrians walk beneath the streets of Montreal every day, enjoying the displays. They find their way around the warren of tunnels thanks to clever maps and signs.

Architects and town planners have even designed beautiful squares and other special features, like fountains, to give the underground space character.

AN UNUSUAL PLACE TO LIVE

The residents of this city can gamble in a casino, attend a church service, and spend their wages in various shops and bars. There is even a hotel, so that tourists can experience the sensation of living underground.

WHERE: the Australian desert.

SKYLINE: on the dry surface there is nothing to see but ventilation shafts surrounded by sand. Everything happens underground.

WHY IT WAS BUILT: as protection against extreme temperatures (blistering heat in summer and cool winters).

INTERESTING FACT: inhabitants live in tunnels previously intended for mining.

SUPERMARKET

COLOR OF THE WALLS

Coober Pedy is rose-colored, not because it is following a fashion trend, but because this is the natural color of the sandstone out of which the city is carved.

DUGOUTS

The dugouts are caves carved out of the earth and refurbished as homes. They tend to be dark, but they are also cozy and quiet—perfect for a peaceful night's sleep!

COOBER PEDY

The name Pedy derives from the aboriginal term *kupa-piti* meaning "white man's hole"; so-called because of all the mining shafts prospectors dug in their search for opals.

Many Europeans came Coober to this part of Australia after the Second World War, keen to make a fortune from mining opals.

RECEPTION

HOTEL

OPAL

Beautiful treasures are hidden in the walls of Coober Pedy. Home improvements—like carving out a tunnel adjoining your dugout—might reveal an iridescent opal (a semi-precious mineral).

THE HIGH LINE. Not everything that stands out above ground in the Big Apple (a nickname for New York) is made of concrete, steel, and glass. Thanks to the High Line, a park created on a former railway line, local residents and tourists can enjoy plants, trees, and fresh air.

BROOKLYN BRIDGE

Pedestrians, drivers, and passengers stream back and forth between Manhattan and Brooklyn across this bridge using many different means of transport. The choice is yours!

THE LOWLINE PROJECT

Being underground doesn't necessarily mean you are cut off from natural light. The Lowline project is a proposal to build the world's largest underground park in the world, using clever technology to transmit sunlight from the surface down below through skylights.

NEW YORK

WHERE: Manhattan, New York (USA)

SKYLINE: Above ground: huge skyscrapers lit up with jewel-colored lights—just like we see in films. Below ground: a subterranean area with equally impressive constructions.

WHY IT WAS BUILT: the hustle and bustle of people (businessmen, tourists, locals and their pets) in the streets of this great metropolis is exhausting; but you can escape, both high above and below ground.

GRAND CENTRAL TERMINAL

It is highly likely that if you travel to New York, you will end up in this vast station where trains enter and leave the city. It is a beautiful building with Cathedral-high ceilings that offers respite from the crowded streets.

SUBWAY

Even though it is over 115 years old, the subway network is still going. It runs 24 hours a day at full capacity. Some of the stations are built as far down as 174 feet below the surface.

PROTECTION AGAINST INVASION

We see huge round stones at certain strategic points in the tunnels. What were they used for? To block passageways at times of invasion and stop the enemy from entering.

VENTILATION SHAFTS

In addition to wells for water, the inhabitants built a sophisticated ventilation system that brought in air from outside, and would win praise from modern engineers.

UNDERGROUND RIVER

The inhabitants chose the location for this subterranean city because a river ran through its subsoil. They built many wells to access it, so if their enemies managed to poison the water in one well, they could still access safe and clean water from another.

DERINKUYU

WHERE: Cappadocia (Turkey)

UNDERGROUND: the long tunnels appear to be endless. There are 18 storeys of them altogether, but only eight can be visited at the moment.

WHY IT WAS BUILT: this ancient city served as a refuge from enemies. Inside, there are kitchens, wells, a church, houses, and stables—everything needed to spend a very long period of time here without coming up to the surface.

THE REASON FOR THE NAME: Derinkuyu means "deep well," which gives us an idea of what we will find here—a lot of water, far below! All the same, it is a surprise to learn that it was a multi-level labyrinth that could house up to 20,000 people.

TUNNEL TO KAYMAKLI

Derinkuyu may have had a 5-mile tunnel connecting it with Kaymakli, another city in Capadocia. Historians believe this was an escape route in case of extreme danger, and a sign that communities helped each other.

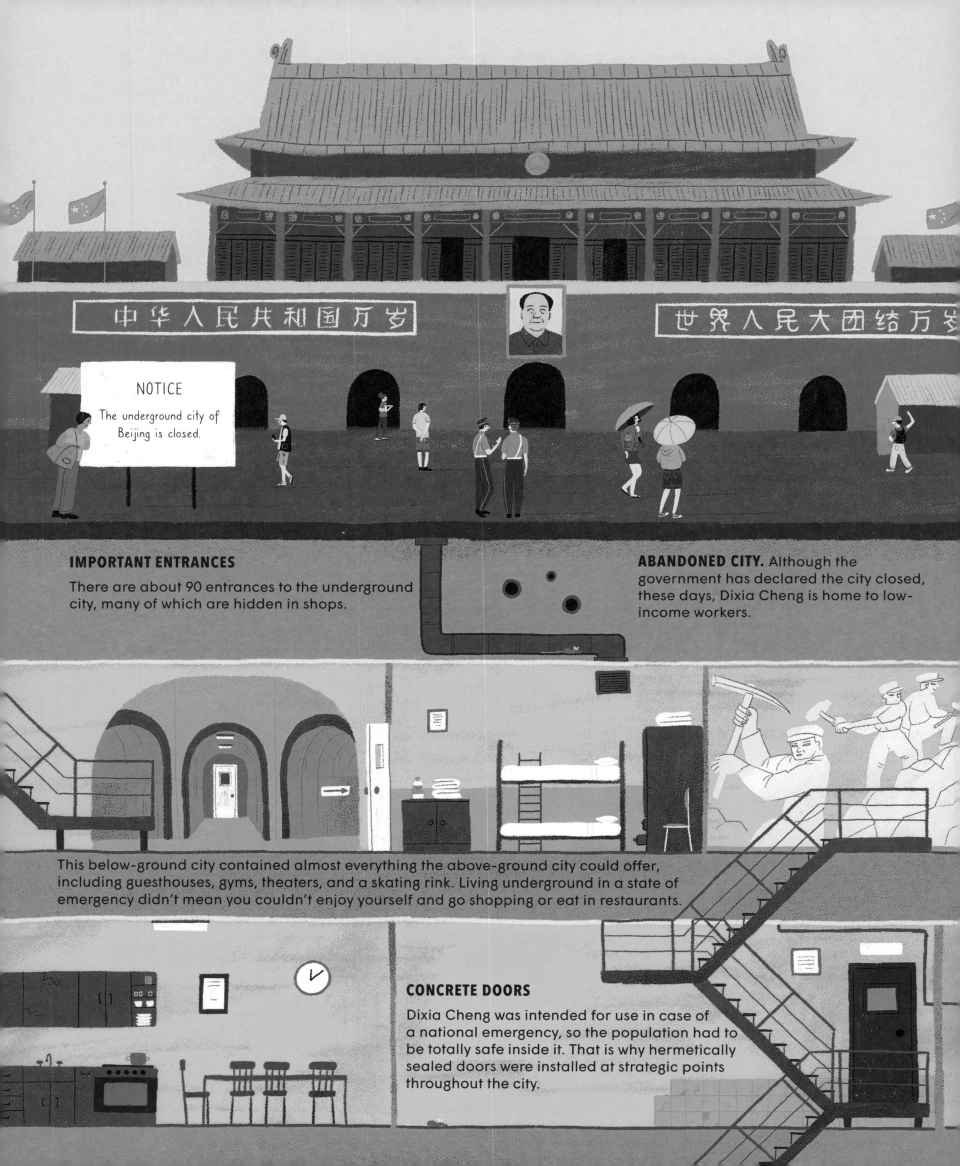

中华人民共和国万岁

世界人民大团结万岁

NOTICE

The underground city of Beijing is closed.

IMPORTANT ENTRANCES

There are about 90 entrances to the underground city, many of which are hidden in shops.

ABANDONED CITY. Although the government has declared the city closed, these days, Dixia Cheng is home to low-income workers.

This below-ground city contained almost everything the above-ground city could offer, including guesthouses, gyms, theaters, and a skating rink. Living underground in a state of emergency didn't mean you couldn't enjoy yourself and go shopping or eat in restaurants.

CONCRETE DOORS

Dixia Cheng was intended for use in case of a national emergency, so the population had to be totally safe inside it. That is why hermetically sealed doors were installed at strategic points throughout the city.

DIXIA CHENG

WHERE: Beijing (China)

WHEN IT WAS BUILT: the 1970s

NAME: Dixia Cheng means "city under the ground" in Chinese.

WHY IT WAS BUILT: In the middle of the Cold War with Russia, China decided to build a city that could withstand a nuclear attack and protect the entire population of Beijing (6 million at the time).

INTERESTING FACT: it never needed to be used.

CULTIVATION / STORAGE. The Chinese thought of everything. If they had to survive shut in here for a long period, they had places to store food and grow crops without sunlight, as well as access to wells and water treatment technology.

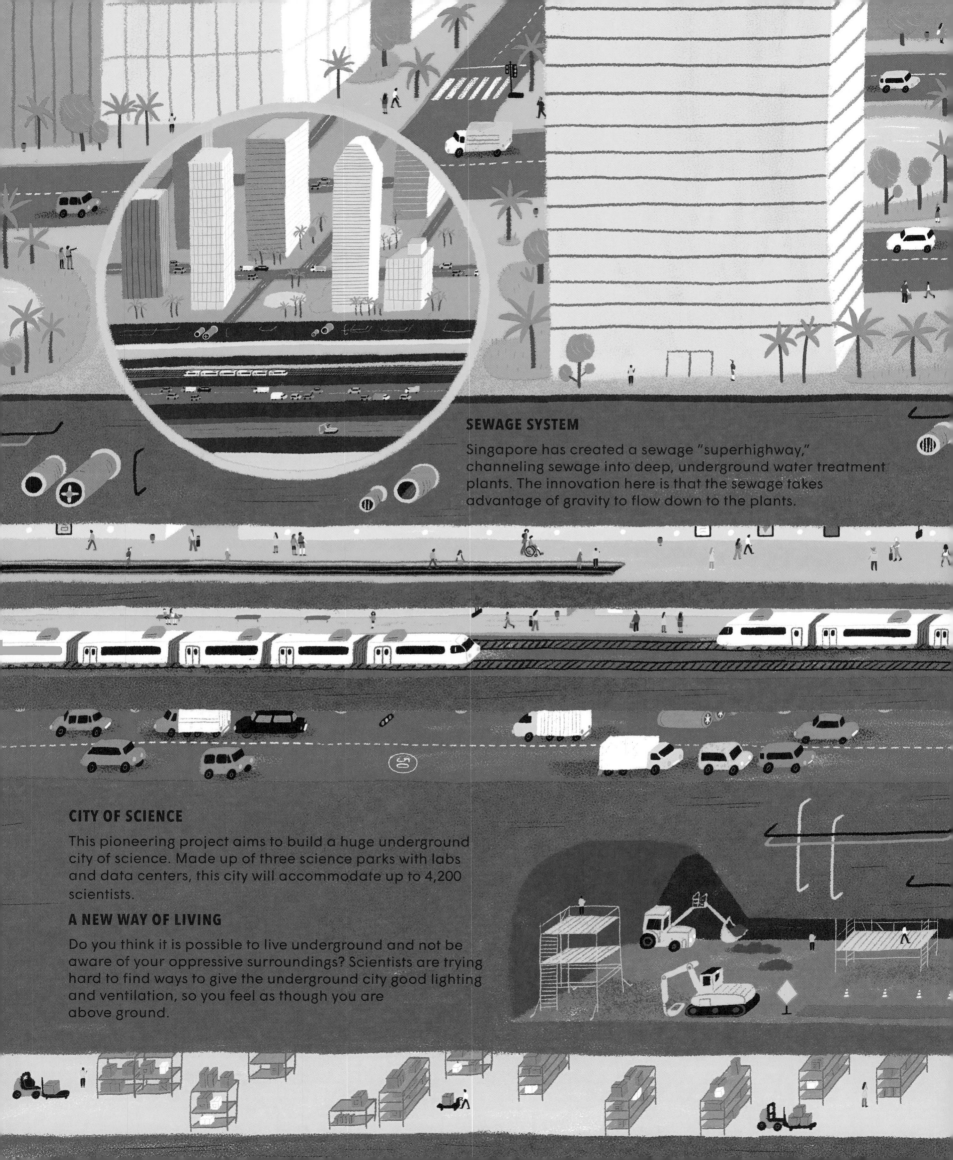

SEWAGE SYSTEM

Singapore has created a sewage "superhighway," channeling sewage into deep, underground water treatment plants. The innovation here is that the sewage takes advantage of gravity to flow down to the plants.

CITY OF SCIENCE

This pioneering project aims to build a huge underground city of science. Made up of three science parks with labs and data centers, this city will accommodate up to 4,200 scientists.

A NEW WAY OF LIVING

Do you think it is possible to live underground and not be aware of your oppressive surroundings? Scientists are trying hard to find ways to give the underground city good lighting and ventilation, so you feel as though you are above ground.

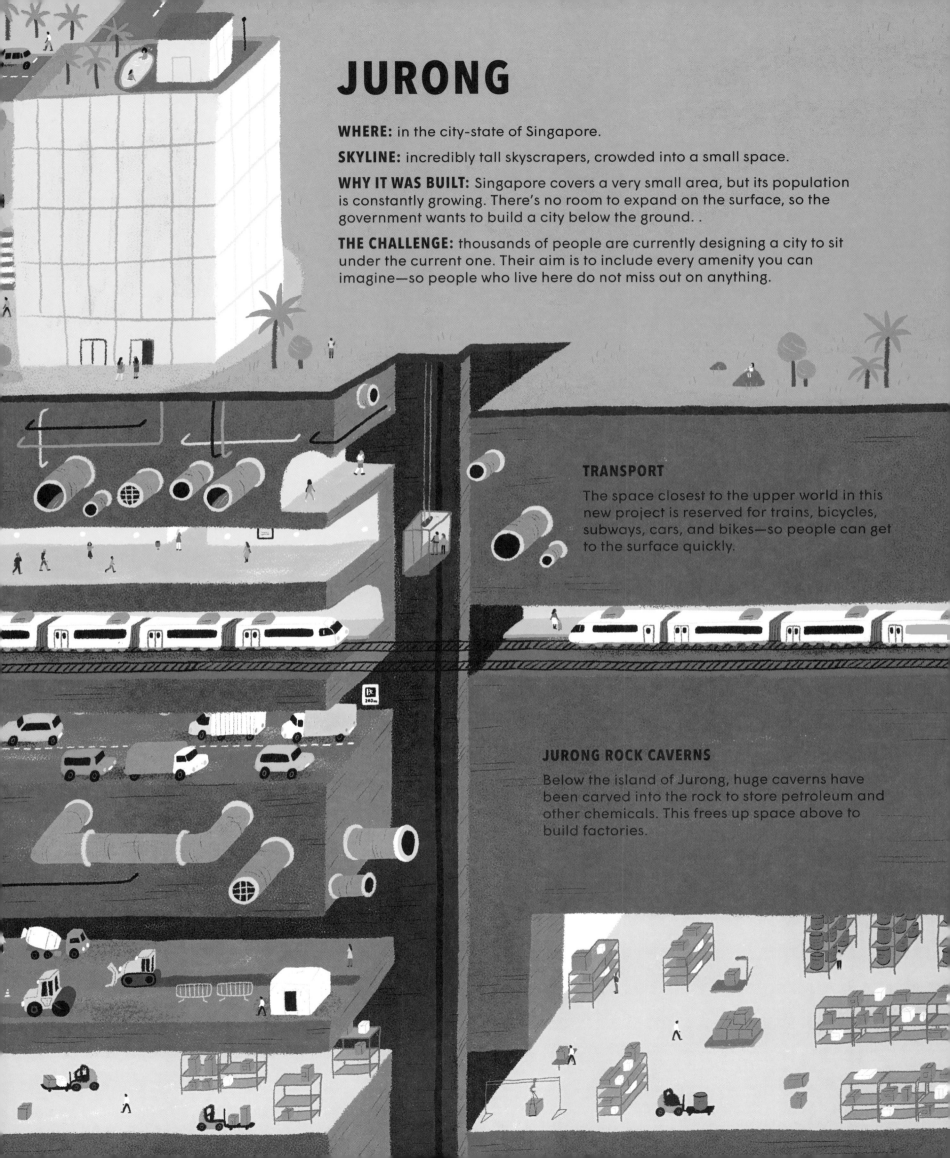

JURONG

WHERE: in the city-state of Singapore.

SKYLINE: incredibly tall skyscrapers, crowded into a small space.

WHY IT WAS BUILT: Singapore covers a very small area, but its population is constantly growing. There's no room to expand on the surface, so the government wants to build a city below the ground. .

THE CHALLENGE: thousands of people are currently designing a city to sit under the current one. Their aim is to include every amenity you can imagine—so people who live here do not miss out on anything.

TRANSPORT

The space closest to the upper world in this new project is reserved for trains, bicycles, subways, cars, and bikes—so people can get to the surface quickly.

JURONG ROCK CAVERNS

Below the island of Jurong, huge caverns have been carved into the rock to store petroleum and other chemicals. This frees up space above to build factories.

WIELICZKA SALT MINE

WHERE: a couple of miles from Krakow (Poland).

SKYLINE: this former mine has 9 levels with more than 186 miles of tunnels and 3,000 chambers. Only 2 miles of it is open to visitors but you can see beautiful chapels and statues carved from salt as well as huge lakes.

WHY IT WAS BUILT: to mine salt, originally discovered here in the 13th century. There's no mining these days, but the underground attraction is now a UNESCO World Heritage Site and a popular tourist destination.

CHAPEL OF SAINT KINGA

This huge chapel, 59 feet high and covering 10,763 square feet, was built in honor of Saint Kinga, the patron saint of salt miners. It is the biggest underground church in the world. The church has excellent acoustics and so concerts and masses are regularly held here.

WINDSURFING ON THE LAKES

In 2004, Mateusz Kusznierewicz, a sailor and winner of many world championship medals, went windsurfing on the deepest lake of the tourist trail. The lake is 29.5 feet deep and situated 459 feet below sea level—and it is completely still. A huge fan had to be brought in to create enough wind for Mateusz to surf.

RECREATION OF THE MINE

Throughout the tourist trail are displays recreating the life and hard work of the miners in the past.

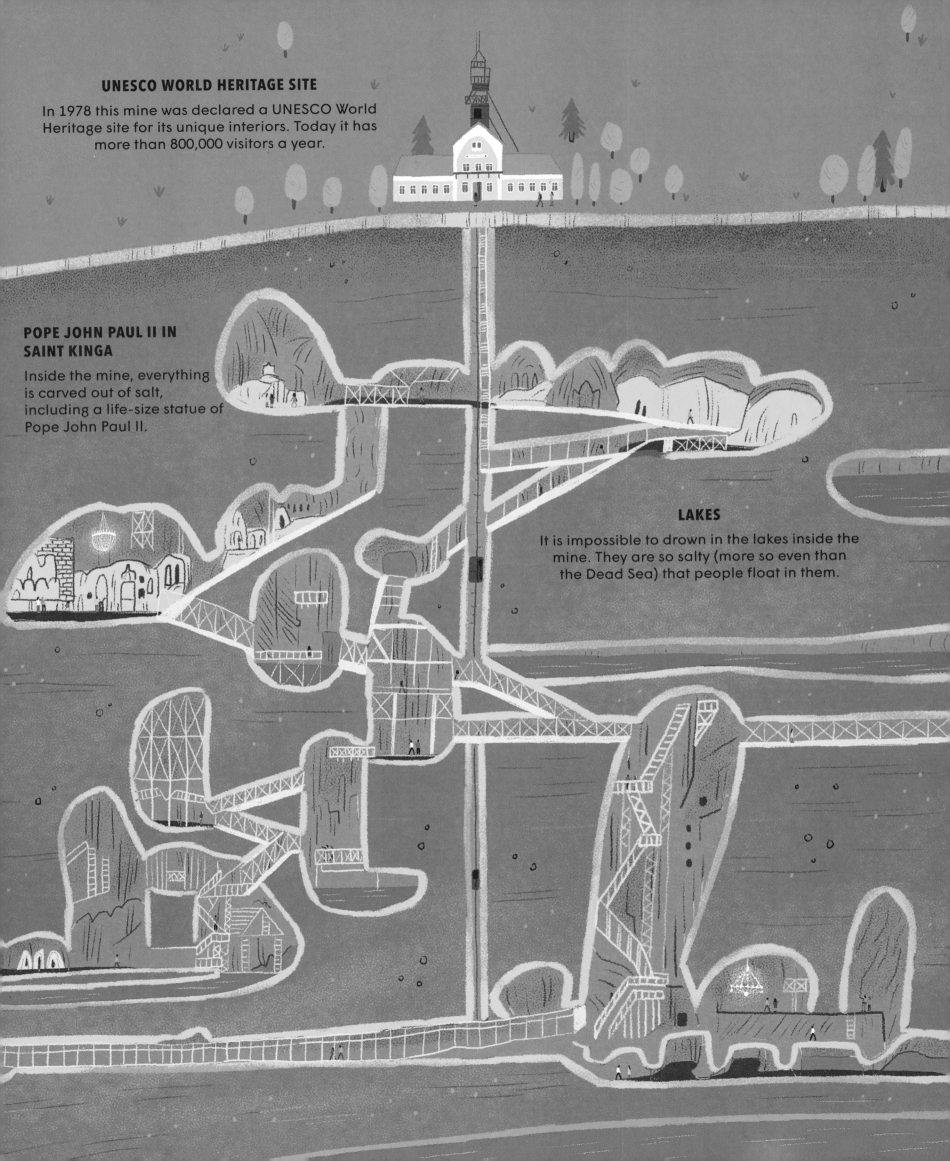

UNESCO WORLD HERITAGE SITE

In 1978 this mine was declared a UNESCO World Heritage site for its unique interiors. Today it has more than 800,000 visitors a year.

POPE JOHN PAUL II IN SAINT KINGA

Inside the mine, everything is carved out of salt, including a life-size statue of Pope John Paul II.

LAKES

It is impossible to drown in the lakes inside the mine. They are so salty (more so even than the Dead Sea) that people float in them.

VOSTOK

WHERE: Antarctica.

SKYLINE: a stark surface, covered in snow, with the largest subglacial lake on the continent beneath it.

INTERESTING FACT: there is almost no life on the surface but there are indications of a vibrant natural city of living organisms in the underground lake. They could have been there for 30 million years.

DISCOVERY: the lake was discovered in 1974 by scientists from the research station of the same name.

WHY IS THERE WATER BENEATH THE ICE?

There may be 2 reasons:

- The pressure of the ice (360 atm) prevents the water from solidifying even though it is at 26.6°F.

- The geothermic heat of the Earth warms the rocks under the lake and acts as an insulating blanket.

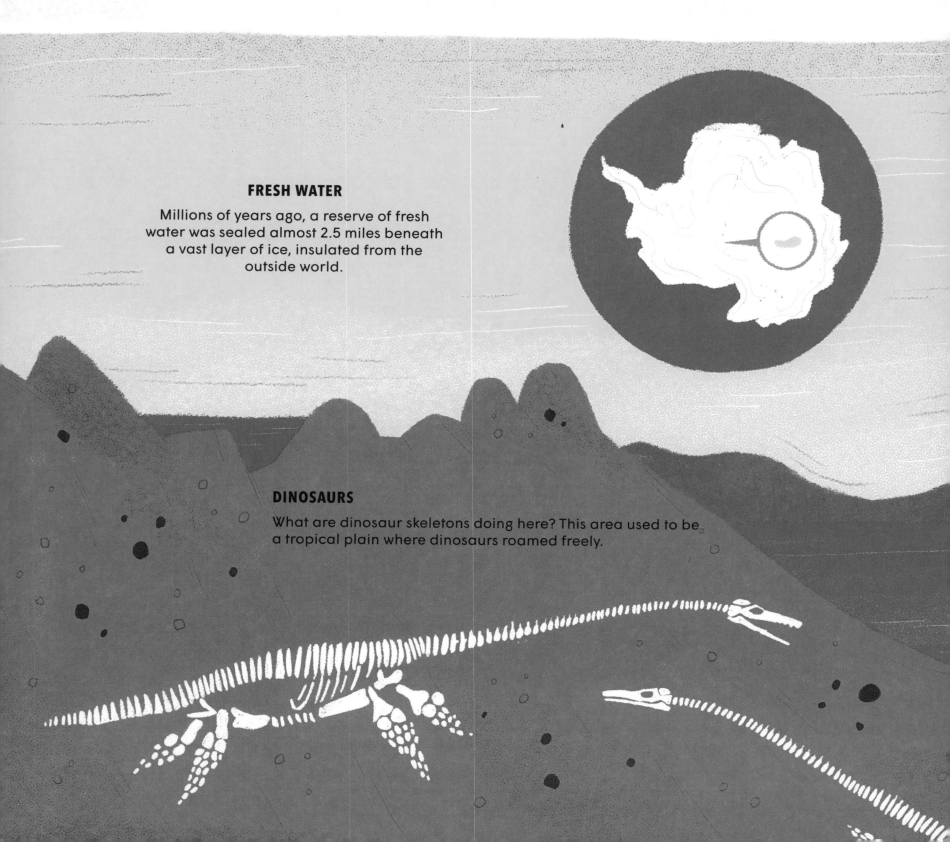

FRESH WATER

Millions of years ago, a reserve of fresh water was sealed almost 2.5 miles beneath a vast layer of ice, insulated from the outside world.

DINOSAURS

What are dinosaur skeletons doing here? This area used to be a tropical plain where dinosaurs roamed freely.

THE RUSSIAN RESEARCH STATION

Vostok is one of the coldest places on Earth.
In 1983 the lowest temperature reached on
Earth was recorded here: -128.6°F. It is a very
inhospitable place to live. Even so, in the summer,
25 scientists and engineers work at the station;
and in the winter, 13 live here.

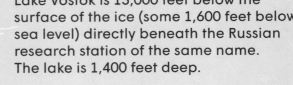

LOTS OF LAKES

The lake isn't unusual. Antarctica has more than
400 subglacial freshwater lakes.

LAKE LIFE

It seems that some simple organisms like
fungi and bacteria are able to live in extreme
conditions, without sunlight.

LOCATION /DEPTH

Lake Vostok is 13,000 feet below the
surface of the ice (some 1,600 feet below
sea level) directly beneath the Russian
research station of the same name.
The lake is 1,400 feet deep.

MAPPING TECHNIQUES

Helicopters fly over the earth, projecting rays from a powerful laser in order to make a 3D map of the hidden city.

SIZE AND POWER OF THE CITY

At the beginning of their investigation, archaeologists thought they were dealing with a small group of houses but later they realized that this city was very large and powerful between the fifteenth and nineteenth centuries. It is believed that up to 10,000 people lived here.

KWENENG

WHERE: Suikerbosrand Nature Reserve near Johannesburg (South Africa)

NOTHING UP ABOVE: The remains of this metropolis are buried deep underground. There is not much to see on the surface, except some broken stone walls, hidden in the flat African veld landscape of dry grass.

WHY IT WAS BUILT: a former settlement and trade center, built over a surface of 7.7 square miles.

Using laser technology, archaeologists have been able to map the lost city from above. In the absence of written records, this discovery adds to our awareness of a period about which little is known in South Africa.

Judging by some demolished houses, it appears that the city was attacked and then abandoned in about 1820 because of various civil wars.

NEW CITY

Yungay lay beneath too much debris to rebuild and the government tried to move the village to another location. However, survivors from the village wanted to stay nearby; so the emergency camp, 0.6 mile north, became the site of the new village.

YUNGAY

WHERE: Yungay, the Highlands of Peru

THE TRAGEDY: In 1970 there was a massive earthquake (8.0 on the Richter scale) that triggered an avalanche of ice and earth from a nearby mountain. As it rushed down the mountain, the ice melted and turned into the mudslide that buried the village of Yungay.

CEMETERY

The cemetery of Yungay, situated on a small rise, escaped the avalanche. This place proved a refuge for the few people who had gone that day to visit their dead. What a sad contradiction.

TRACES OF THE BURIED CITY

Even today, a visit to Yungay is overwhelming. Little remains of the once bustling village: a single bell tower stands out, the collapsed church and the cemetery. Nature has reclaimed the site, which has been designated a national cemetery, creating a peaceful memorial.

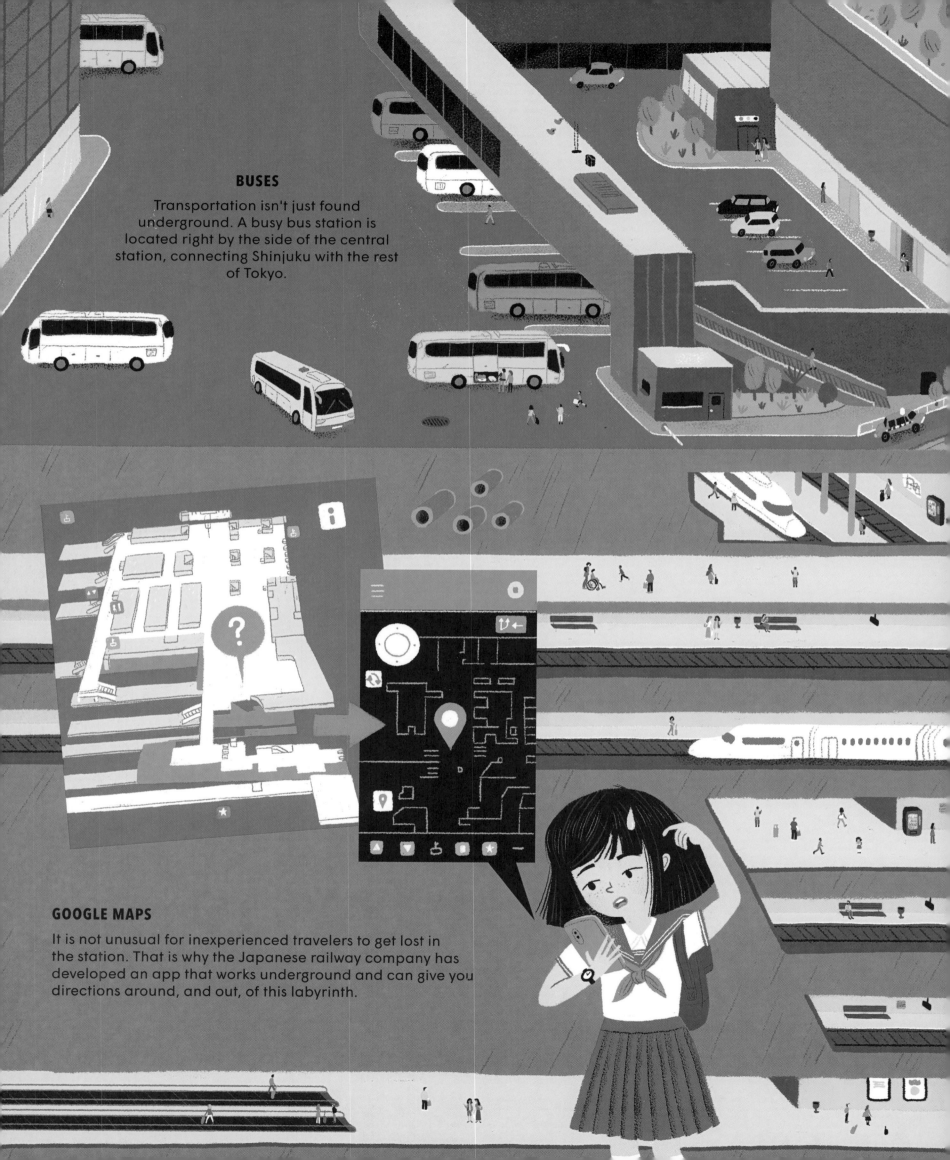

BUSES

Transportation isn't just found underground. A busy bus station is located right by the side of the central station, connecting Shinjuku with the rest of Tokyo.

GOOGLE MAPS

It is not unusual for inexperienced travelers to get lost in the station. That is why the Japanese railway company has developed an app that works underground and can give you directions around, and out, of this labyrinth.

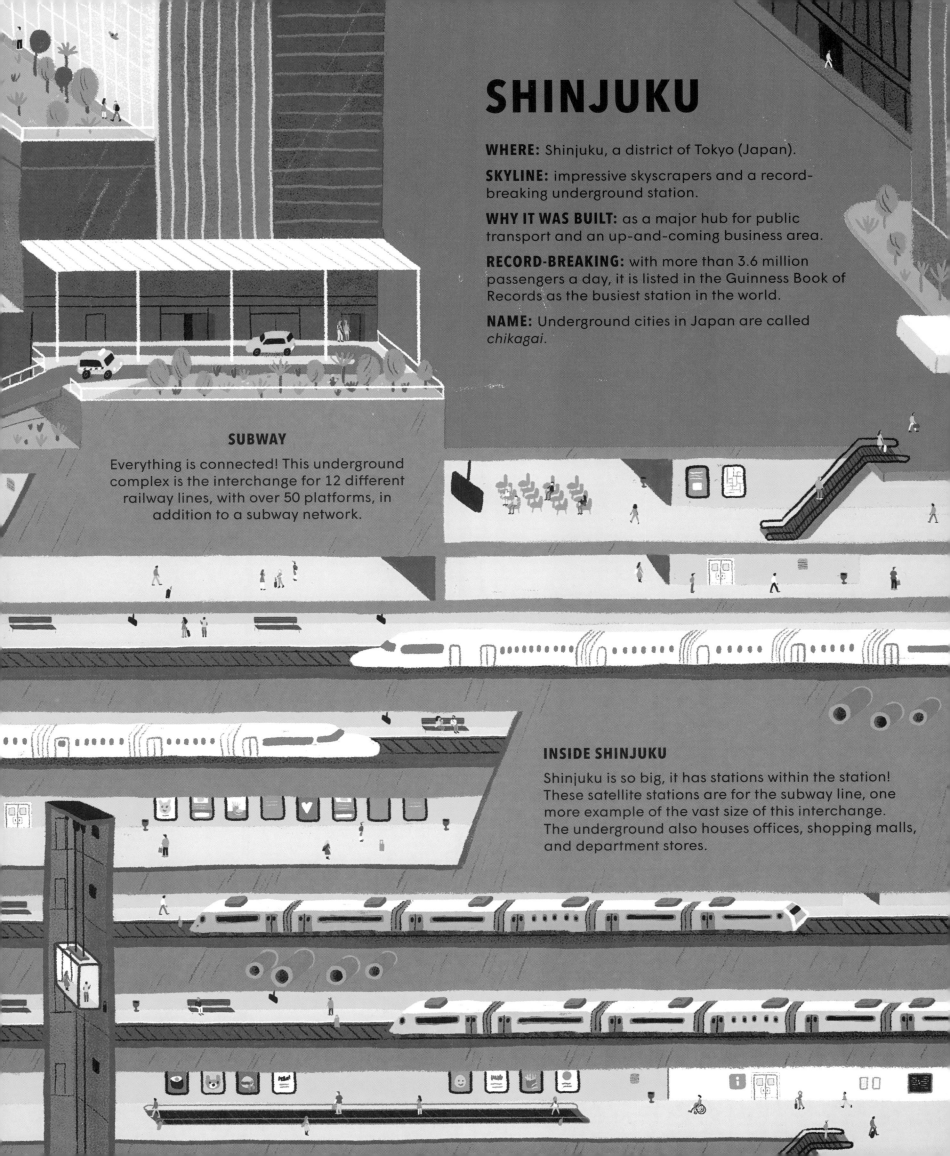

SHINJUKU

WHERE: Shinjuku, a district of Tokyo (Japan).

SKYLINE: impressive skyscrapers and a record-breaking underground station.

WHY IT WAS BUILT: as a major hub for public transport and an up-and-coming business area.

RECORD-BREAKING: with more than 3.6 million passengers a day, it is listed in the Guinness Book of Records as the busiest station in the world.

NAME: Underground cities in Japan are called *chikagai*.

SUBWAY

Everything is connected! This underground complex is the interchange for 12 different railway lines, with over 50 platforms, in addition to a subway network.

INSIDE SHINJUKU

Shinjuku is so big, it has stations within the station! These satellite stations are for the subway line, one more example of the vast size of this interchange. The underground also houses offices, shopping malls, and department stores.

PYRAMID OF GIZA

WHERE: Giza Plateau (Egypt).

SKYLINE: situated on the west bank of the Nile, this area of Giza has three impressive pyramids, palaces, and temples—as well as the Great Sphinx.

IMPORTANCE: the Great Pyramid of Giza is more than 4,000 years old and the largest man-made building ever constructed: 479 feet by 754 feet at the base. It was built as a tomb for Pharaoh Khufu, and contains passageways leading to chambers deep inside.

INTERESTING FACT: Giza is not strictly speaking a city, but a necropolis (a burial complex). This one was created for several Pharaohs, other royal family members, and government officials.

NECROPOLIS

Here, we can visit two other large pyramids—one of which was for Khufu's son, Pharaoh Khafre, and a few small pyramids which are thought to be for Khufu's wife and mother; as well as some temples, and the world-famous Great Sphinx statue.

BURIAL BOAT

The Egyptians believed in an afterlife. When they died, the Pharaohs were buried together with items they would need to rule in the Underworld, including a boat symbolizing their journey there.

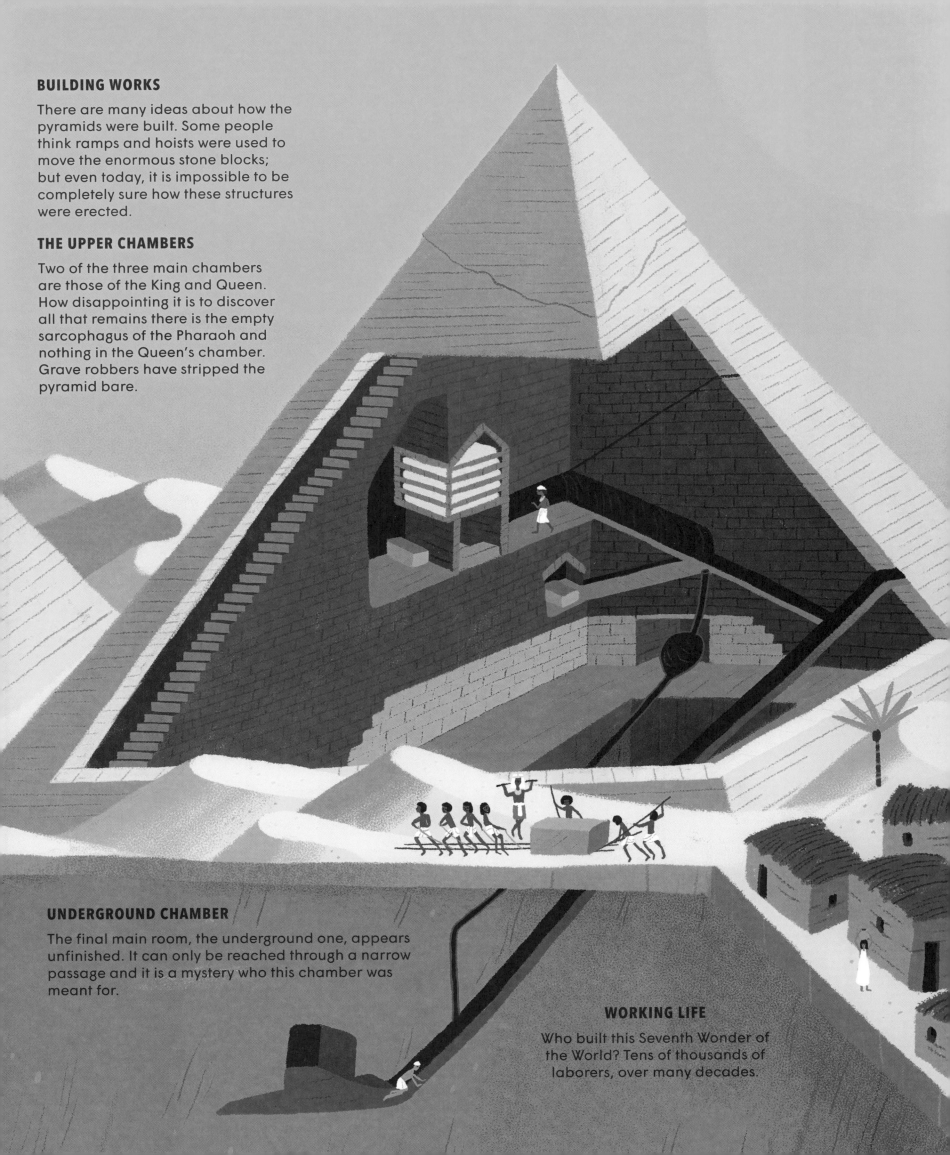

BUILDING WORKS

There are many ideas about how the pyramids were built. Some people think ramps and hoists were used to move the enormous stone blocks; but even today, it is impossible to be completely sure how these structures were erected.

THE UPPER CHAMBERS

Two of the three main chambers are those of the King and Queen. How disappointing it is to discover all that remains there is the empty sarcophagus of the Pharaoh and nothing in the Queen's chamber. Grave robbers have stripped the pyramid bare.

UNDERGROUND CHAMBER

The final main room, the underground one, appears unfinished. It can only be reached through a narrow passage and it is a mystery who this chamber was meant for.

WORKING LIFE

Who built this Seventh Wonder of the World? Tens of thousands of laborers, over many decades.

THE RIVER LIFFEY

The River Liffey divides the city into north and south, and used to represent a social class division: north for the working class and south for the well-to-do.

THE LAGOON

This is the site of the black lagoon, where the Vikings moored their boats.

RIVERS AND STREAMS

Although there are more than 60 streams under the ground, it is impossible to see them as they are hidden under streets and buildings.

DUBLIN

WHERE: Dublin (Ireland)

SKYLINE: a fairly small city, situated on a bay and easily explored on foot or by public transport.

WHY IT WAS BUILT: as a Viking base for raids on the rest of Ireland.

ORIGIN OF THE NAME: Dublin (Dubh Linn "black lagoon").

CONTRASTS: a city full of bustle on its surface but with little life underground.

SOGGY UNDERGROUND

The composition of the soil and high levels of underground water, from rivers and aqueducts, make building underground difficult. At the moment trams, buses, and trains still operate on the surface.

PLANS FOR A METRO

There are plans to build the city's first underground metro. However, many believe it won't be possible. How will Dublin cope with its growing population and congested roads?

THE TEMPLE BAR

BAR

UNDERGROUND TOURISM

Located 66 feet below ground, and spread across 200 miles of tunnels, the catacombs are a big draw for inquisitive tourists who refuse to leave the city without exploring its surprising entrails.

THE CATACOMBS

The Catacombs were constructed because Paris' cemeteries were too full. The bones of as many as 6 million Parisians rest in these ossuaries.

RESERVOIRS

This lovely turquoise lake, which looks good enough to bathe in, provides enough drinking water for a fifth of the population of Paris.

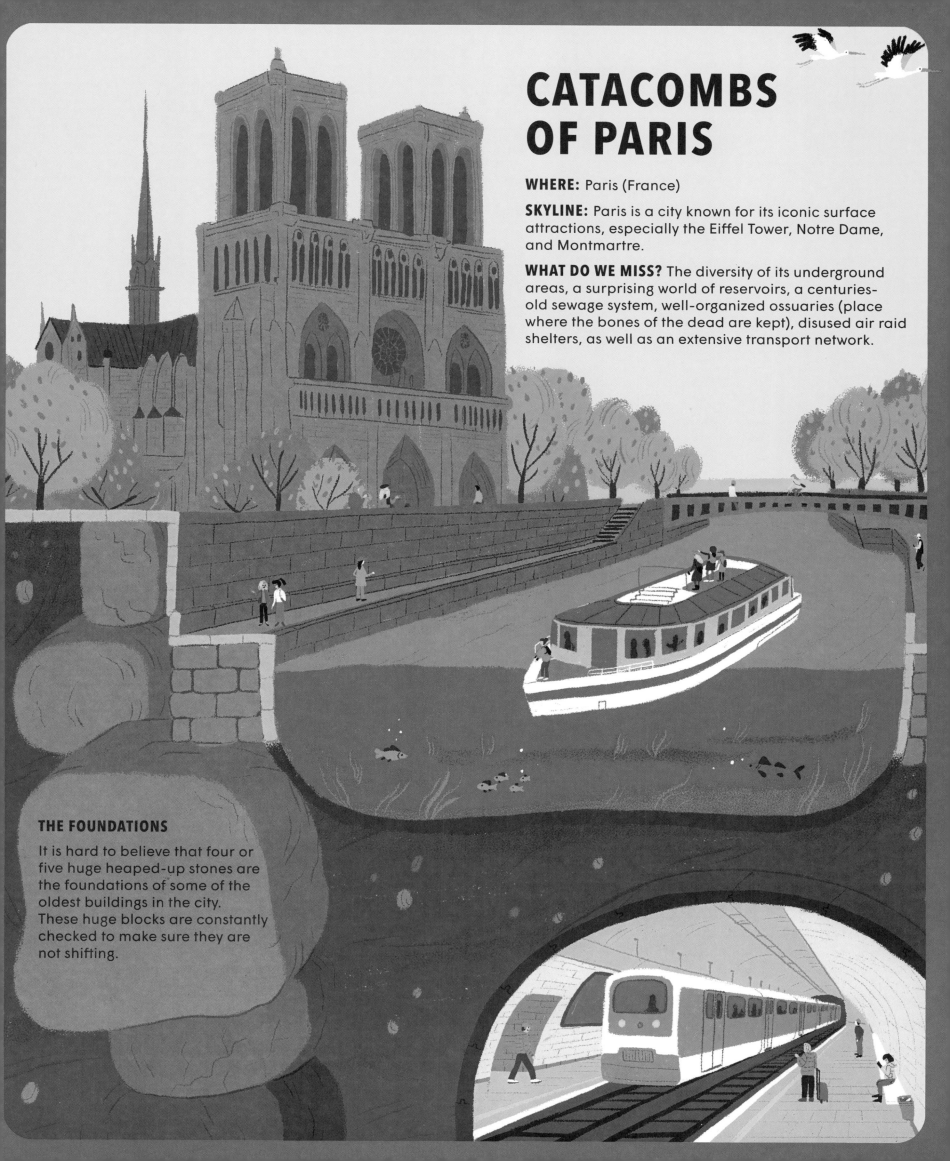

CATACOMBS OF PARIS

WHERE: Paris (France)

SKYLINE: Paris is a city known for its iconic surface attractions, especially the Eiffel Tower, Notre Dame, and Montmartre.

WHAT DO WE MISS? The diversity of its underground areas, a surprising world of reservoirs, a centuries-old sewage system, well-organized ossuaries (place where the bones of the dead are kept), disused air raid shelters, as well as an extensive transport network.

THE FOUNDATIONS

It is hard to believe that four or five huge heaped-up stones are the foundations of some of the oldest buildings in the city. These huge blocks are constantly checked to make sure they are not shifting.

ICEWORM

TUNNEL BENEATH THE SNOW IN GREENLAND
WHAT IT WAS INTENTED FOR: nuclear missile storage.

The project, known as Iceworm, was an attempt to store nuclear missiles beneath the ice in Greenland; ready to fire in defense during war. The project was canceled.

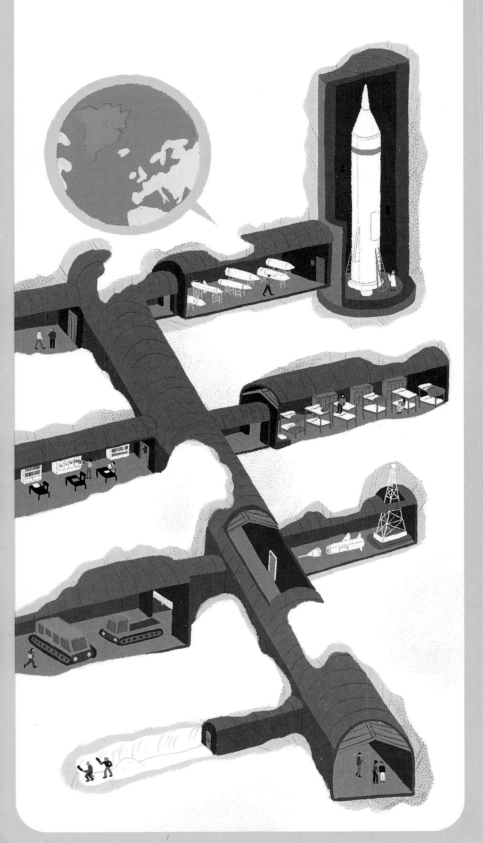

CHANNEL TUNNEL

UNDERWATER TUNNEL BETWEEN FRANCE AND THE UNITED KINGDOM
WHY IT WAS BUILT: to connect two countries.

It is one of the longest submerged tunnels in the world, allowing travelers to reach France or the United Kingdom in half an hour. Its total length is 31.35 miles. 23 miles of them are submerged, and it was built in 1994.

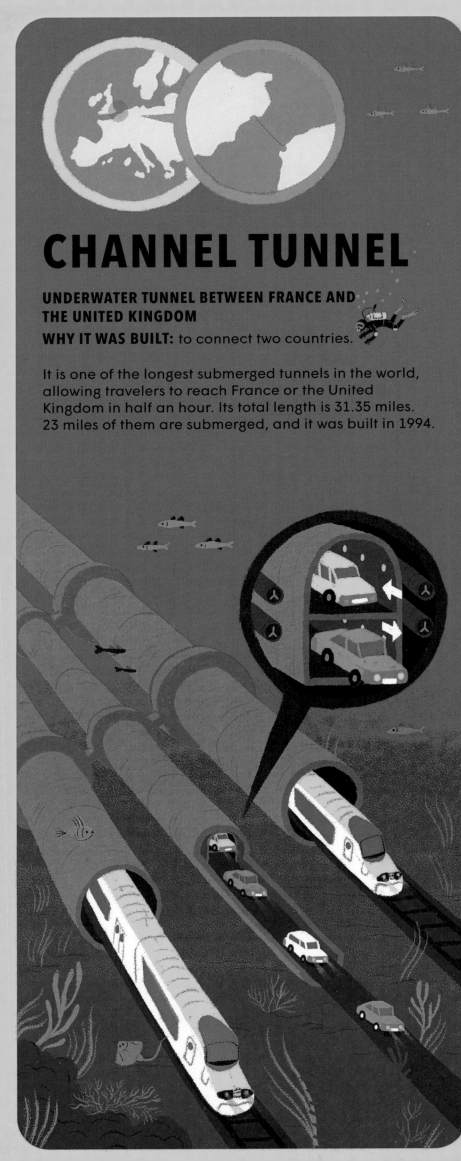

TURKSTREAM

SUBMERGED TUNNEL BETWEEN TWO CONTINENTS
WHY IT WAS BUILT: to transport gas.

Few Europeans know that the gas they use for cooking, heating, and so on comes from Russia. It is transported through a pipeline that for 565 miles of its length passes beneath the Black Sea. It is a project of enormous significance, especially strategically.

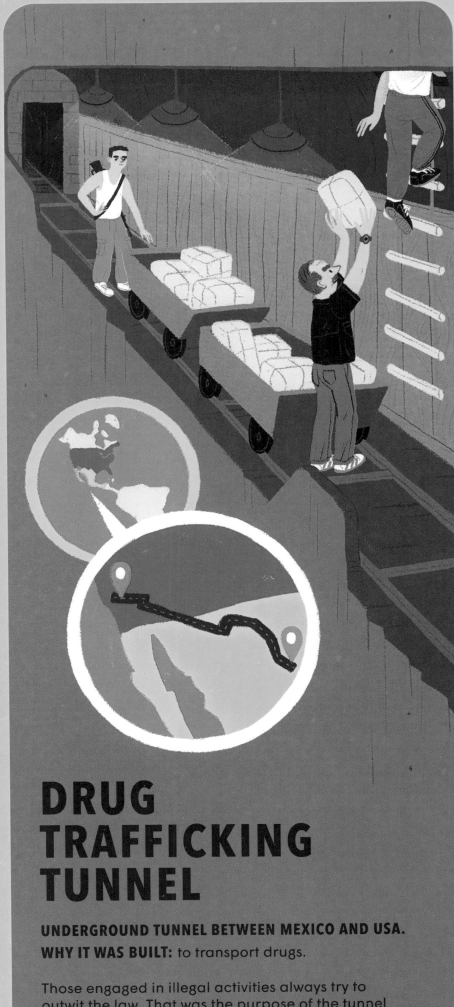

DRUG TRAFFICKING TUNNEL

UNDERGROUND TUNNEL BETWEEN MEXICO AND USA.
WHY IT WAS BUILT: to transport drugs.

Those engaged in illegal activities always try to outwit the law. That was the purpose of the tunnel connecting Tijuana (Mexico) and San Diego (USA), dug by smugglers to evade police checks. In order to transport the drugs quickly, they laid rails in the tunnel and used mine carts.

BARCELONA

WHERE: Barcelona.

SKYLINE: a city with tall buildings on the surface, nestling between the sea and the mountains, and with a vibrant history.

A VERY DIVERSE UNDERGROUND AREA: transport, shelters, ancient ruins, dance clubs and many other interesting venues.

BÀRCINO

Bàrcino, an ancient Roman city, has been excavated and is ready to be visited. Would you like to live like a Roman for a while? Visit the baths and the wine cellar or stroll through ancient streets.

MOVING BUILDINGS

This palace looks as if it has been here forever, doesn't it? In fact, construction work on the Via Laietana began in 1930 and involved many buildings being transferred, stone-by-stone, to another part of Barcelona.

AIR RAID SHELTERS

When the air raid alert sounded during the war, everyone ran to the shelters. Some had to reach them from the street, like the one which is found in the Plaza del Diamante. Others were lucky enough to have a private entrance from their house, as in the Pedrera.

SUBWAY

If you are lucky enough to visit Barcelona, we urge you to take the subway. Keep your eyes open and you will see a number of ghost stations, such as Gaudí, which although ready for use was never opened.

GAUDÍ